Birds of Prey

Johanna Rohan

Contents

Birds of Prey

Birds of **prey** are strong
hunters. They catch and kill
other animals to eat.

Dino Name!
Birds of prey are
also known as
raptors.

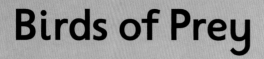

Small Males

Mostly, female
birds of prey
are much larger
than males.

Bald Eagle

There are around 300 **species** of birds of prey in the world. They can be sorted into groups.

These groups are:

ospreys

eagles

vultures

kites

falcons

owls

hawks

5

Birds of prey have excellent eyesight, hearing and smell. These **senses** help them to search for and hunt their prey.

Eye Spy

A Bald Eagle's eyesight is so good it can see a fish while flying hundreds of metres above the water.

The Turkey Vulture can smell and find food even while flying high in the air.

Barn Owls can find their prey in the dark using their amazing sense of hearing.

Birds of prey have strong, powerful feet with curved, sharp **talons**. This helps them to catch, hold and kill their prey.

back talon

Sharp Talons
A falcon's back talons are so sharp they could cut through your wrist!

Birds of prey have very sharp beaks shaped like hooks. This helps them to stab and rip meat.

Clever Feet

Birds of prey use their feet, not their beaks, to catch their prey.

Eagles

Eagles are very powerful birds of prey. They have large beaks, huge feet and talons, and big **wingspans**.

Up High
Eagles build their nests in tall trees or on high cliffs.

Golden Eagle

Eagles

Size:	very large birds of prey
Diet:	fish, lizards, snakes, other birds, and even monkeys, pigs and goats!
Lifespan:	around 30 years in the wild

The Wedge-tailed Eagle

One of the world's largest eagles can be found in Australia – the Wedge-tailed Eagle. These eagles have wedge-shaped tails, and wingspans of 2.5 metres.

Dinner Time
Wedge-tailed Eagles can form a team to hunt large animals.

Wedge-tailed Eagle

Hawks

Hawks have long tails and short, rounded wings.
They can fly quickly and steer sharply.

Types of Hawks

Harriers and Buzzards are types of hawks.

a Harrier

a Buzzard

Hawks

Size:	medium-sized birds of prey
Diet:	small mammals, reptiles, insects and sometimes other birds
Lifespan:	around 25 years in the wild

The Goshawk

The Goshawk has short, broad wings with a wingspan of 1.2 metres. Its long tail helps it fly swiftly through the forest.

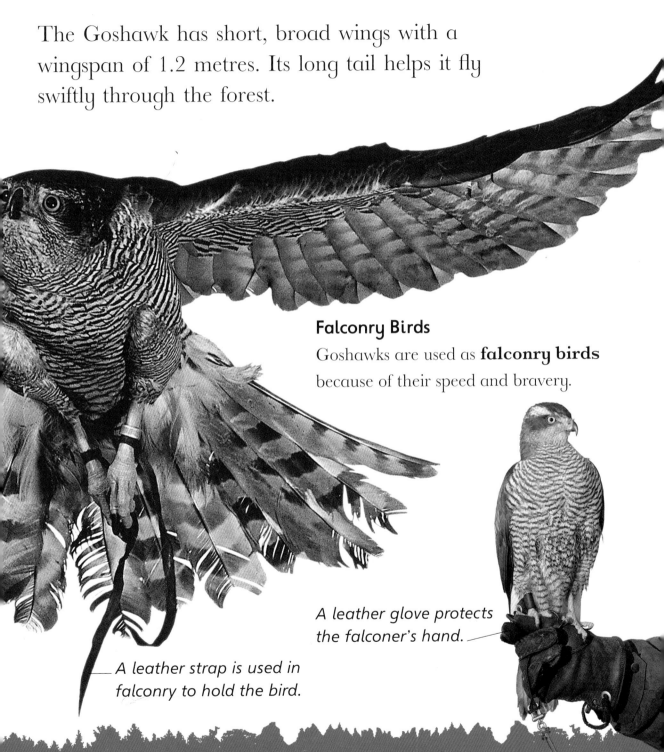

Falconry Birds

Goshawks are used as **falconry birds** because of their speed and bravery.

A leather glove protects the falconer's hand.

A leather strap is used in falconry to hold the bird.

Falcons

Falcons have long pointed wings to help them fly at high speed and change direction quickly.

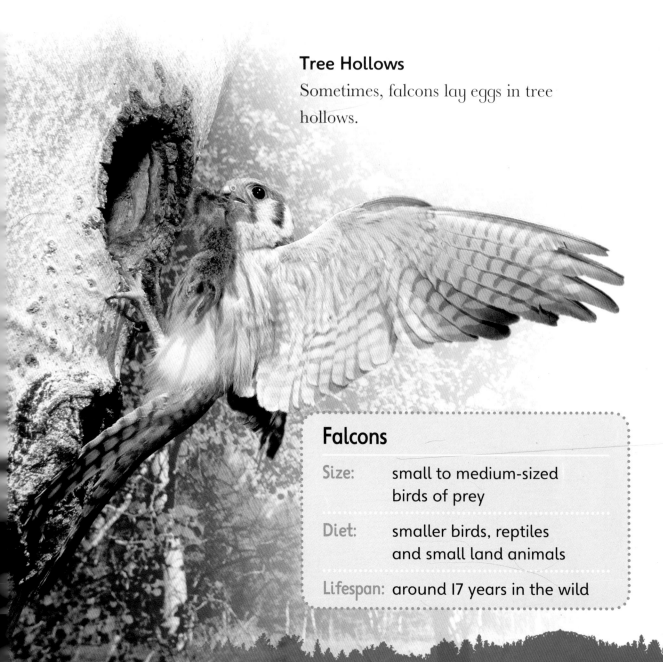

Tree Hollows

Sometimes, falcons lay eggs in tree hollows.

Falcons

Size:	small to medium-sized birds of prey
Diet:	smaller birds, reptiles and small land animals
Lifespan:	around 17 years in the wild

The Peregrine Falcon

The Peregrine Falcon is the fastest animal on Earth. It hits prey at high speed in the air. This kills the prey.

1.2 metre wingspan

High-speed Flyer

The Peregrine Falcon can fly at speeds of over 400 km per hour. That's as fast as the fastest train on Earth!

Ospreys

Ospreys are found all over the world near lakes, rivers and seas.

The Osprey is sometimes called the Sea Hawk.

Osprey

Size:	large birds of prey
Diet:	fish
Lifespan:	around 30 years in the wild

Catching Prey

The Osprey flies slowly over water, looking for its prey. When it sees a fish, it **hovers**. Then it dives feet first into the water to grab it. It can close its nostrils and dive up to one metre underwater!

Good Grip

Ospreys have rough pads on their feet. This helps them to grab slippery fish!

17

Kites

Kites are found in warm areas around the world. They glide and **soar** through the air and quickly **swoop** to catch their prey.

The Black-shouldered Kite

The Black-shouldered Kite is a small, pale-grey raptor found in Australia. Black-shouldered Kites mostly eat mice. But they will also eat grasshoppers, rats and even rabbits.

Kites

Size:	small, light birds of prey
Diet:	insects, small animals and even dead animals
Lifespan:	around 20 years in the wild

Black-shouldered Kites have wingspans of just under one metre.

Owls

Owls are **nocturnal** birds of prey found around the world. They have flat faces, small hooked beaks and large eyes that face forwards. Most owls only hunt at night.

Down in One!

Most owls swallow their prey whole. Then they spit out any fur, feathers or bones.

African Great Horned Owl

Owls

Size:	small to medium-sized birds of prey
Diet:	small animals, insects, other birds and fish
Lifespan:	around 60 years in the wild

The Snowy Owl

The Snowy Owl is found in the Arctic. It keeps warm with thick feathers, even on its feet and toes.

Snowy Owls get their name because they are almost pure white.

Hunting All Hours

It does not get dark in the Arctic summer so Snowy Owls can hunt in the day or night.

Vultures

Vultures have long, broad wings. This helps them soar long distances for food. Vultures are **scavengers**. They do not often kill their own prey.

Vultures

Size:	very large birds of prey
Diet:	dead or dying animals
Lifespan:	most vultures live for around 30 years in the wild, although Andean Condors can live to 60.

The Andean Condor

The Andean Condor is a vulture. It's one of the largest flying birds in the world. It has a wingspan of over 3 metres!

Andean Condors eat large dead animals, such as deer or cattle.

Bald Head

Vultures have bald heads. If vultures had head feathers, they would get spattered with blood when they ate dead animals. This would be very hard to clean!

Endangered Birds of Prey

About 25 types of birds of prey around the world are **endangered** because of:

- **habitat loss**
- **poaching**
- **pollution.**

The Californian Condor is a very endangered species.

Habitat loss has meant some birds of prey have lost their homes.

Some endangered birds of prey around the world are:

Philippine
Eagle

Crowned Eagle

Philippine Eagle
Egyptian Vulture
Crowned Eagle
Indian Vulture

Egyptian Vulture

Indian Vulture

The Californian Condor

The Californian Condor is close to **extinction**. Over the years, people have shot or poisoned many of them.

The Californian Condor has a huge wingspan of around 3 metres.

Is It a Bird? Is It a Plane?

Californian Condors have been mistaken for small aeroplanes because they are so big when they soar!

Californian Condor

Size: one of the largest birds of prey

Diet: dead animals, such as cattle and deer

Habitat: rocky scrubland, forests and savannas

Lifespan: around 50 years

In 1990, there were no Californian Condors left in the wild. People wanted to help, so Californian Condors were **bred** in zoos and wildlife parks. Some birds have been set free, back into the wild.

Today, there are around 300 Californian Condors left in the world.

Caring for Chicks

This chick was bred in a zoo. A puppet that looks like an adult Condor is used to care for it. The chick thinks the puppet is its mother!

Saving Birds of Prey

There are many ways to help save endangered birds of prey.

1. Birds are being bred in zoos and wildlife parks.

2. People look after the wild places where birds of prey live.

3. Zoos and wildlife parks are teaching people about birds of prey.

Helping Hand
A vet is helping this Condor chick to hatch at a zoo.

This falconer is teaching school children about birds of prey.

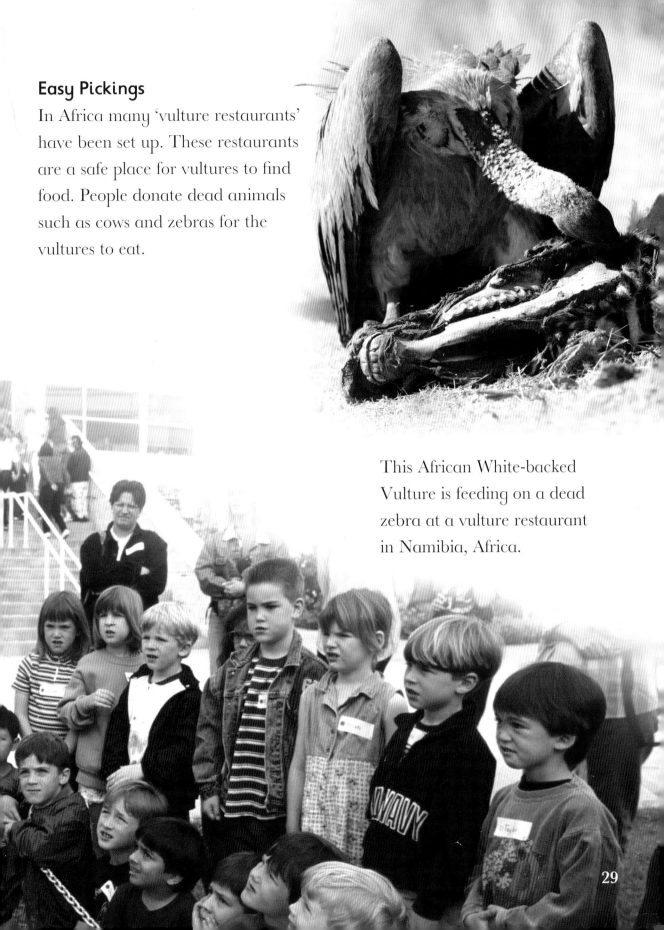

Easy Pickings

In Africa many 'vulture restaurants' have been set up. These restaurants are a safe place for vultures to find food. People donate dead animals such as cows and zebras for the vultures to eat.

This African White-backed Vulture is feeding on a dead zebra at a vulture restaurant in Namibia, Africa.

It's Quiz Time!

Here are five questions to test your bird of prey knowledge. The answers are on page 32 – good luck!

Question 1
What is another name for a bird of prey?

Question 2
True or false? Male birds of prey are usually larger than the females.

Question 3
What type of bird of prey is used as a falconry bird?

Question 4
What is the fastest animal on Earth?

Question 5
True or False? The Andean Condor is a type of vulture.

Northern Goshawk

Glossary

bred
made chicks

endangered
when an animal species is in danger
of extinction

extinction
when a species of plant or animal
dies out forever

falconry birds
birds of prey trained for the sport
of falconry

habitat loss
destruction of an animal's home

hovers
floats in the air

nocturnal
active at night

poaching
killing an endangered species

pollution
things that harm the environment

prey
animal hunted, killed and eaten by
another

scavengers
animals that feed on dead animals

senses
animal's sight, hearing and smell

species
group of animals that are alike

soar
fly high in the air

swoop
to fly down upon something

talons
claws of birds of prey

wingspans
lengths of birds' wings,
from tip to tip

Index

Quiz Answers
Question 1: a raptor
Question 2: false
Question 3: the Goshawk
Question 4: the Peregrine Falcon
Question 5: true